JEFF GNASS
HAWAII
MAGNIFICENT WILDERNESS

PHOTOGRAPHY AND TEXT BY JEFF GNASS

WESTCLIFFE PUBLISHERS, INC. ENGLEWOOD, COLORADO

CONTENTS

International Standard Book Number:
ISBN 0-942394-38-0
Library of Congress Catalogue Card Number:
86-062901
Copyright, Photographs and Text: Jeff Gnass, 1987
Designer: Gerald Miller Simpson/Denver
Typographer: Edward A. Nies
Printer: Tien Wah Press (Pte.), Ltd., Singapore
Publisher: Westcliffe Publishers, Inc.
2650 South Zuni Street
Englewood, Colorado 80110

First frontispiece: Nanue Stream descends amid a tropical forest, Hamakua Coast, Island of Hawaii

Second frontispiece: Surf action at dusk in Keawalai Cove, Island of Maui

Third frontispiece: Rain clouds and surf designs on the North Kohala Coast, Island of Hawaii

Title page: Palms beside ancient Alii Fishpond, Island of Molokai

Right: Afternoon clouds build over Anaehoomalu Bay, South Kohala Coast, Island of Hawaii

PREFACE

A dazzling sun commands every season; clouds veil forested summits; ribbons of water disappear into jungles; seas pound at lava cliffs; giant volcanoes reach into the troposphere — these scenes are the quintessence of the Hawaiian landscape.

I first went to Hawaii in 1968. That "visit" lasted nearly seven years; ten more would pass before my return. But I went back with an entirely different purpose — one of exploring this island landscape with camera and lens. In those intervening years my life had taken on new direction. During my absence I had also developed an awareness about the natural world. Now, as a photographer, and with an eye trained to see the spectacle of wilderness, I was drawn back to Hawaii to make a personal, visual statement about this special place.

The Hawaiian chain is one of the youngest land forms on Earth. Primarily submerged, this long string of seamounts and shield volcanoes stretches 1,600 miles across the Pacific floor. Intermittently it emerges from the tropical seas in the form of islands and atolls. The Hawaiian Islands are situated on the eastern end of this underwater mountain chain and are the most recent formations along its extent. Geologists estimate the islands are between one and five million years old — youthful in the paradigm of plate tectonics. Here, modern man can observe, first-hand, the very primal stages of a land-building process that continues to define the veneer of our planet.

Elements of change predominate in these Islands: fleeting twilight punctuates the days; eternal seas whiten the margins; billowing clouds become mountain showers; sunset skies fade to starry nights — these are the rhythms of Hawaii I remember. Once engrossed in its

cycles again, I quickly became attuned to my subject, so important for sincere expression in any art.

This portfolio of images is a distillation of my impressions of Hawaii's land and sea. The visual chaos that so often interferes with our ability to perceive our surroundings has been excluded by the framing of the camera. For a moment, each photograph narrowly focuses attention on a single aspect of the landscape. Collectively then, these vignettes of a larger realm show us a view of that entire world. Thus is my intention with these photographs and they stand on their own toward that end.

With each photography trip, I endeavor to seek out new expressions of the land. Hawaii is a place of many contrasts. At times this challenges the capabilities of color photography, especially when carried out with the large-format. Years ago I settled on the 4″ × 5″ format view camera as my primary camera. This image size provides the subject fidelity I demand and supports a comfortable rhythm working in the field. But choosing this format has its price. Imposing weight, bulky equipment, reduced mobility — these are some of the consequences I have accepted. Probably the hardest factor to overcome is a loss of spontaneity. Dramatic events in the landscape seldom last more than several minutes at best. Through years of living in the outdoors, I've become adept at predicting the ephemeral moment.

An example is the picture on pages 72-73 of sunset on the Na Pali Coast. I'd visited this vantage point off the coast trail several times before in pursuit of a dramatic photograph. When I headed down the trail that stormy afternoon, my expectations weren't high. A few large raindrops started falling and the weather became even more foreboding. Upon arriving at my

Gendarmes of the palm grove guard a stretch of coral beach, South Kona Coast, Island of Hawaii

location, a sliver of clear sky was visible under the dark roof of clouds. My hopes weren't entirely erased and I quickly set up the tripod and camera and mounted a lens. From past experience with equatorial sunsets, I estimated this one wouldn't last much longer than a minute. Poised with light meter in hand, camera ready and film holder inserted, I waited restlessly. Ten seconds for light readings, I figured, and time yet to expose several sheets of film. Then it happened — the sun peeked out beneath the clouds and the most spectacular sunset light I've ever seen flooded across the surface of the ocean below. The light almost seemed to come forth in puffs as the rays lit the ocean spray. In my awe I nearly missed making the exposures and then it was over in little more than 60 seconds. The film captured only a hint of the presence I felt while I was surrounded by this moment.

For me the most satisfying activity in photographing nature is exploring new subjects. It is true that the camera and lens do not lie. But in the hands of the unskilled, they do not reveal either. The most difficult skill to develop in photography is composition, or framing the picture. Once a scene has been found, the most important step in composition is selection of the viewpoint. Precise alignment of the camera is then necessary to convey the perspective. But most of my usual working day is spent searching for and revisiting vantage points for the grand landscape. These long ventures provide me with the opportunity for discovery.

Many of my most intimate photographs come about this way. The bizarre close-up of eucalyptus bark on page 84 is one case. I'd known of this superb grove of eucalyptus along the Hana Coast for some time. One rainy day while searching out waterfall pictures in the area, I decided to examine them closer for a possible portrait (I've always been fascinated with trees as subjects). They were located near the bottom of a steep gulch. As I started down the rain-soaked bank, my footing immediately gave way under the saturated topsoil. My mountaineering instincts took over and I found myself in an ungainly glissade on slippery plants and mud. Luckily, I didn't have the tripod and camera over my shoulder as I usually do, or the situation would have been more clumsy. When I finally arrested my descent, I was face-to-face with exotic bark patterns all around me. It was almost startling as my mind was still reeling from the sudden burst of activity. The photo opportunity was obvious. I promptly climbed out of the gulch and soon was back with the camera. It took more than an hour's work in the drizzle on the steep, unstable slope, to set up and make my exposures, but the results were well worth the effort. A subject like this is a fine reward for a day in the field.

When I photograph in a new landscape, it's difficult to concentrate at first because there are so many unfamiliar elements. But soon an intimacy develops, and I begin to feel a unity with my surroundings. This harmony is strengthened when I pause along the way and look more closely at the details of my "new neighborhood."

It is utterly important for us to cultivate a more compassionate fellowship with other living creatures and develop respect for the land with attitudes the equal of the sanctity of the life it supports. Books like this one provide windows to the simple beauty around us. I hope these views will advance awareness and respect for all natural wonder, of Hawaii and the Earth.

With Aloha,

Jeff Gnass

In memory of Carol, who gave me another kind of vision.

Monstera plants crowd before Rainbow Falls, on Wailuku River, Island of Hawaii

MORNING LIGHT

Waimea Canyon fills with morning light, Island of Kauai

Haleakala National Park, Island of Maui:

Sunrise defines Kamoalii and Kalahaku Pali
inside Haleakala crater

Volcanic aggregate and Kupaoa plants on the
rim of Haleakala

Overleaf: Billowing cumulus at sunrise, from
Haleakala's summit

Palm ranks on the South Kona Coast, Island of Hawaii

Sunrise accents the fluted walls of Waimea Canyon,
Island of Kauai

Morning pastels and gentle surflines await the
harsher light of day, at Baldwin Beach with the West
Maui Mountains, Island of Maui

Surf, sand and beach boulders, Hanalei Bay,
Island of Kauai

Fountain grasses ablaze in morning sunlight, North Kona District, Island of Hawaii

The arid slopes of Naio Gulch look across Auau Channel at West Maui, Island of Lanai

Overleaf: Tidepool rocks greet an effulgent sunrise, near Kealia, Island of Kauai

Ioa Needle catches morning sunlight — Ioa Stream
cascades below, Island of Maui

Cascade of Uluhe ferns, in the Hoary Head Range,
Island of Kauai

Amaumau ferns on the brink of Kilauea Caldera —
Halemaumau steams below, Hawaii Volcanoes National
Park, Island of Hawaii

Banyan tree roots spread in serpentine fashion,
Liliuokalani Park, Island of Hawaii

Overleaf: Koolau Range and the Windward Coast, from
Nuuanu Pali, Island of Oahu

Coral reef and beach detail, at Kuau Cove,
Island of Maui

Boulders populate a tidal area, near Kealia,
Island of Kauai

MOTION

*Foaming surf and wet sand designs, at Wainiha Bay on
the Hanalei Coast, Island of Kauai*

Wailuku River floods the Boiling Pots, Island of Hawaii

Ocean spray explodes over rocks in Hulopoe Bay,
Island of Lanai

Wave action on the Waianae Coast, Island of Oahu

Halawa Stream pursues its course below Lower Moaula Falls, Island of Molokai

Overleaf: Surf crashes on coastal rocks in afternoon's dazzle, at Puu O Kaiaka, Island of Molokai

Surging sea and volcanics along Keanae Peninsula,
Hana Coast, Island of Maui

Rain-swollen Oheo Gulch, Haleakala National Park,
Island of Maui

*Kalakaoo Stream plummets over Akaka Falls, Hamakua
Coast, Island of Hawaii*

Spouting Horn blows into a sunset sky, Island of Kauai

*Overleaf: Surf patterns and intertidal
rocks in Anaehoomalu Bay, South Kohala Coast,
Island of Hawaii*

Saltwater spills from lava headlands, at Puu Pehe Cove,
Island of Lanai

Wailua Falls unveils on a grotto wall, lower slopes of
Haleakala, Island of Maui

DAY LIGHT

Oleander plants and stone wall in upland country, on
Hualalai, Island of Hawaii

Palms line Kaimu Black Sand Beach, on the Puna Coast,
Island of Hawaii

Ohia tree shares a Kalalau Valley vista from Kokee,
Island of Kauai

Kipahulu District, Island of Maui:

Wailua Falls disappears into the jungle forest on Haleakala

Breakers in Pepeiaolepo Bay, Haleakala National Park

Overleaf: Arch Rock and black sea cliffs in Pailoa Bay, Hana Coast, Island of Maui

Exposed reef and surf runoff on Papohaku Beach,
Island of Molokai

Miniature stream in bamboo and tree fern forest,
Hamakua Coast, Island of Hawaii

Opaekaa Falls below Makaleha Mountains,
Island of Kauai

Lava pavement and scattered coral stretch before palms,
South Kona Coast, Island of Hawaii

*Seawater accents Sweetheart Rock, at Puu Pehe Cove,
Island of Lanai*

*Dried Palapalai ferns in a Koa forest, at Kipuka Ki,
Hawaii Volcanoes National Park, Island of Hawaii*

*Overleaf: Surf and clouds in symphony at Barking Sands
Beach, Island of Kauai*

Hala trees frame Lumahai Beach, Hanalei Coast,
Island of Kauai

Rain forest ground cover, Ioa Valley, Island of Maui

CONTRAST

Palms before morning clouds over Kauai Channel, at Kapaa Beach, Island of Kauai

Shore boulders and surf action on the North Kohala Coast, at Pololu Valley, Island of Hawaii

Harsh landscapes:

Boulder-strewn hills at Garden of the Gods,
Island of Lanai

Ohia forest relics and Devastated Area on Puu Puai,
Hawaii Volcanoes National Park, Island of Hawaii

Fountain grasses invade a Pahoehoe lava field,
North Kona District, Island of Hawaii

Kapuaiwa Coconut Grove beside calm waters, at
Kiowea Beach, Island of Molokai

Pastel sunset beyond breaking surf and rocks, at
Waimea Bay, Island of Oahu

Morning glory and grasses, lower slopes of Hualalai,
Island of Hawaii

MICROCOSM

*Eucalyptus bark minutia, in a jungle forest on Haleakala,
Island of Maui*

*Coconut palms and fronds, South Kona Coast,
Island of Hawaii*

*Amau fern community, on the rim of Kilauea crater,
Hawaii Volcanoes National Park, Island of Hawaii*

*Overleaf: New growth reaches from an Uluhe fern
thicket, Hana Coast, Island of Maui*

Sea, reef and beach rocks, at Kuau Cove, Island of Maui

*Pahoehoe lavafall gleams in morning sunlight,
at Holei Pali, Hawaii Volcanoes National Park,
Island of Hawaii*

EVENING LIGHT

A regal twilight settles on Hulopoe Bay, Island of Lanai

Ohia trees under sunset clouds, at Holei Pali, Hawaii
Volcanoes National Park, Island of Hawaii

Ragged coves and saltwater basins record twilight,
Island of Kauai

Sunset moods:

Palm figures frame Lanai across Auau Channel,
Island of Maui

Eventide reflections from Pahoehoe lava surface,
Holei Lava Field, Hawaii Volcanoes National Park,
Island of Hawaii

*Flooding surf and sea level reflections, Barking Sands
Beach, Island of Kauai*

*Silverswords glow with sunset above the clouds, Haleakala
National Park, Island of Maui*

*Overleaf: Aa lava and coral rubble rims Anaehoomalu
Bay, South Kohala Coast, Island of Hawaii*

Folds in Pahoehoe lava frozen in volcanic time,
Holei Lava Field, Hawaii Volcanoes National Park,
Island of Hawaii

Sea and clouds advance on Barking Sands Beach,
Island of Kauai

Shoreline at Yokohama Bay — Kaena Point in the distance, Island of Oahu

Hapuu tree ferns grace an Ohia forest, upper slopes of Kilauea, Hawaii Volcanoes National Park, Island of Hawaii

Overleaf: Sky and clouds model sunset's colors over Kealaikahiki Channel, Island of Maui

TECHNICAL
INFORMATION

The photographic images in this book were made with a Toyo 4″ × 5″ field view camera and focused with Nikkor lenses with focal lengths of 65mm, 90mm, 135mm, 210mm, and 360mm.

Exposures were calculated with a Pentax 1-degree spot meter and supplemented with both averaging and incident light readings taken with a Gossen Luna Pro SBC. Warming filters were occasionally used to correct the color cast in deep shade. Lens apertures ranged from f/11 to f/64 and shutter speeds varied between 1/30 of a second and 45 seconds.

Kodak Ektachrome 64 daylight transparency film was used exclusively.

Sunset lingers beyond Niihau across Kaulakahi Channel, from Kekaha Beach, Island of Kauai